INCHWORM
AND
A HALF

BY ELINOR J. PINCZES
ILLUSTRATED BY
RANDALL ENOS

SCHOLASTIC INC.

New York Toronto London Auckland Sydney
Mexico City New Delhi Hong Kong Buenos Aires

With love to Grandma's treasures: Hannah
Kuchinsky, Dennis Pinczes, Mac Stannard,
Alec Stannard, and Casey Stannard —E.J.P.

For my grandchildren, Klay and Blake —R.E.

ISBN 0-439-44710-0

12 11 10 9 8 7 6 5 4 3 2   3 4 5 6 7 8/0

Printed in the U.S.A.   08

First Scholastic printing, March 2003

The text of this book is set in 14-point Clarendon.

The illustrations are linocuts with colored overlays.

The inchworm who lives in the garden
can climb any surface with ease.
She nibbles and measures all her treasures—
zucchini, eggplants, and snow peas.

Her measuring method is simple:
each loop that she takes is one inch.

She starts at one end, and results will depend
on the number of loops — that's a cinch!

"Squirmy, wormy, hoopity-hoop!
I measure everything, loopity loop:

2-inch hot peppers and 3-inch pole beans,
and even the tiniest 1-inch new greens."

One day the unthinkable happens:
"My measurement's off just a bit.
One, two, nearly three! How could this be?
There's no way I can possibly fit."

"What's nearly three?" asked a short worm,
who suddenly dropped from mid-air.
"Well," said the worm, starting to squirm,
"Two inches and that fraction there."

"Fractions," the inchworm continued,
"are equal parts of a whole number.

It spoils my fun if a length can't be done,
like the end of that problem cucumber."

The little worm grinned. "I'm a fraction,
that length should be easy for me."

He said, sounding wise, "At just half your size,
I'm a one-half-inch fraction, you see."

They happily measured all morning
while fuzzy green leaves made them laugh.

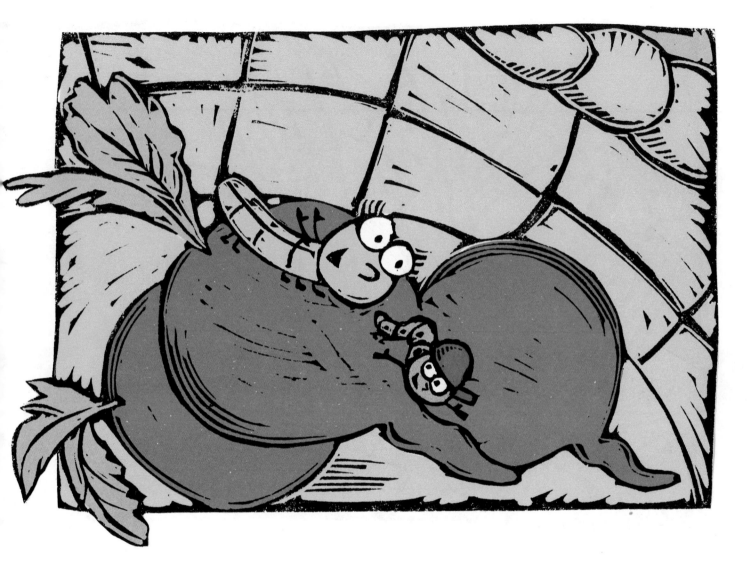

The inchworm said, "One!" and her part was done.
Then the little worm looped, "And a half!"

"Squirmy, wormy, hoopity-hoop!
We measure everything, loopity loop:

7-inch celery, 8-inch corn ears,
and 4½-inch asparagus spears."

For every loop made by the inchworm,
the shorter worm had to make two.

Then something went wrong as they inched along—
a measurement they couldn't do!

They carefully studied the problem:
"This fraction is smaller than me,"
said the half-size in total surprise.
"What length could it possibly be?"

Another worm looped to their rescue.
"It looks like you're in a tight spot.
I'll give that a try—I'm little and spry,
and my length's one-third inch on the dot."

The trio looped on into noonday,
quite pleased no new problems occurred.

The inchworm yelled, "Two! That's all I can do!"
Then the shortest worm called, "And a third!"

"Squirmy, wormy, hoopity-hoop!
We measure everything, loopity loop:
8-inch leaf lettuce, 9-inch cabbage head,
and some 1⅓-inch ripe berries, so red."

To equal one loop by the inchworm,
the second worm had to loop twice.
For accuracy, the third worm looped three.
"I'm a one-third-inch fraction, how nice!"

Snacking on rich, ripe tomatoes,
they decided to measure a few.

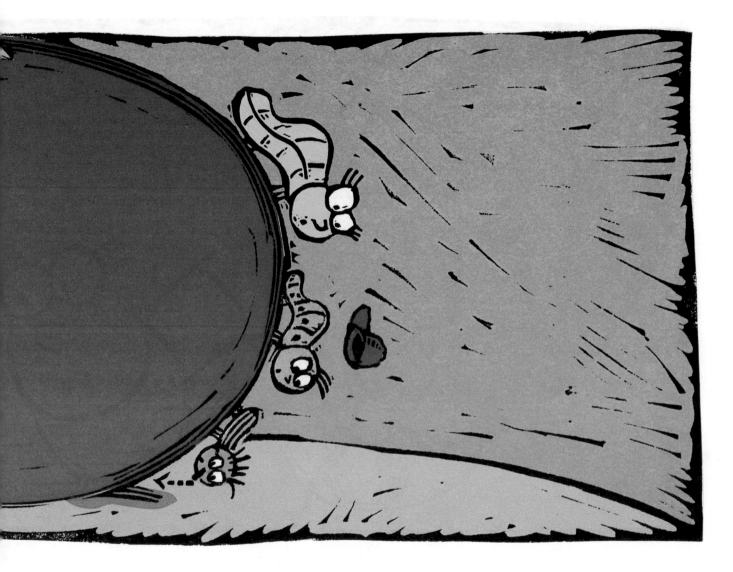

But just like before, they halted once more
at a measurement they couldn't do.

The fraction they saw was a strange one.
"Too short for half-size," they agree.

"How very absurd! Not even one-third.
What length could it possibly be?"

"It's me," said a worm slightly shorter.
He looped off the leaf where he'd curled.

"My four steps per inch make one-fourth a cinch.
Now together we'll measure the world."

"Squirmy, wormy, hoopity-hoop!
We travel everywhere, loopity loop:
No problem's too big, no fraction too small.
By adding new worms, we can measure it all!"